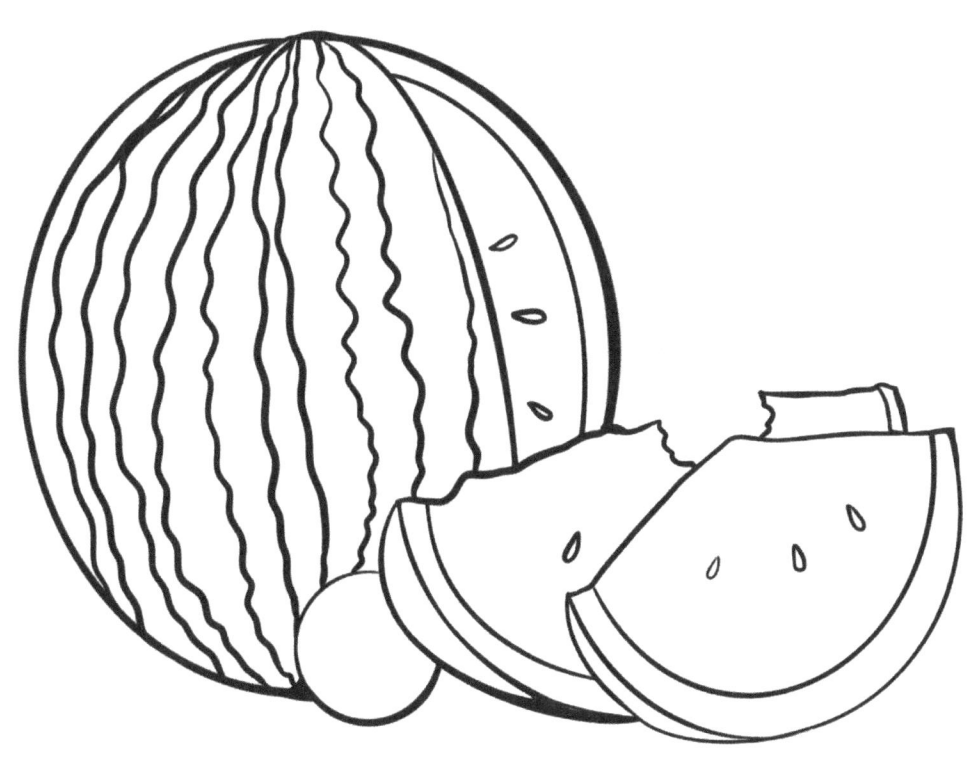

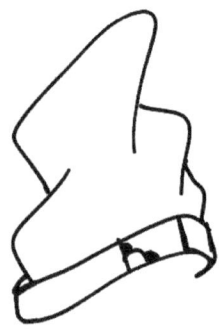

Printed in the USA
ISBN-13: 978-1546341772
ISBN-10: 1546341773

Dedicated to the Culture

Poetic literature inspired by:
"Strange Fruit" a poem by Abel Meeropol
Sung by Nina Simone, Billie Holiday (Sampled by Ye)

Flow inspired by "One Fish Two Fish" by Dr. Seuss

Coloring Book Illustrated & Curated by Manda Pandie

Shout out to God
Shout out to the universe, you know who you are.
☐

Welcome to the Panda coloring community!
We are all about inclusion here.

How to use this book:

There is really no wrong way to use this coloring book.

If you feel a line is disconnected, connect the line.
If you feel like there are too many lines grab some white out.

BTW I encourage everyone to draw outside the lines as well as in between the lines.

Remember to sign your signature after you have finished your masterpiece

& Don't forget to Share your art online and tag me Manda Pandie

@mandapandieillustrations

mandapandie.org

#StayUp #StayConnected #SpreadLove

Can't wait to see your art on the web or on a wall near you <3

From root to leaf
     From leaf to root
These southern trees have
     such...

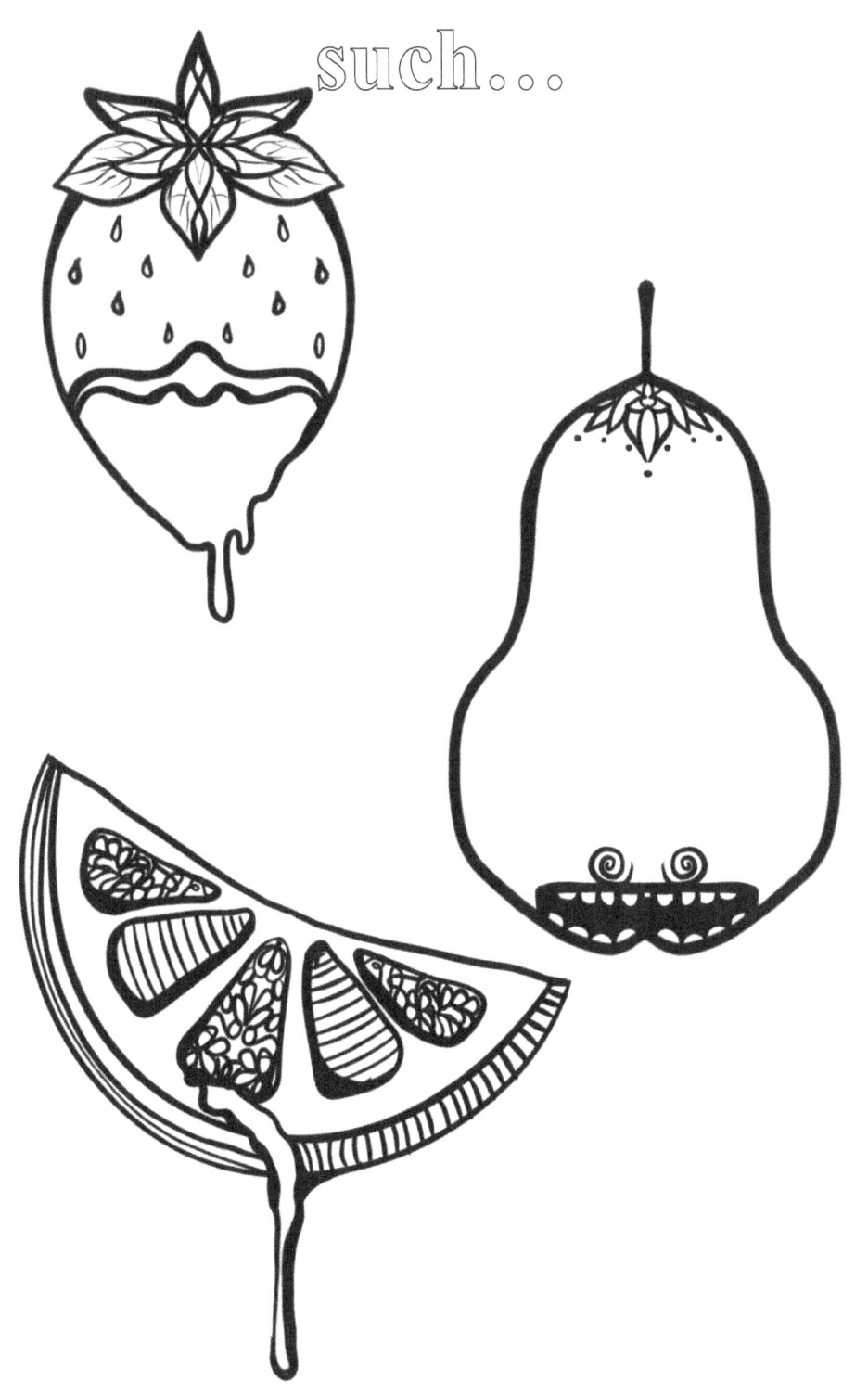

Strange fruit.

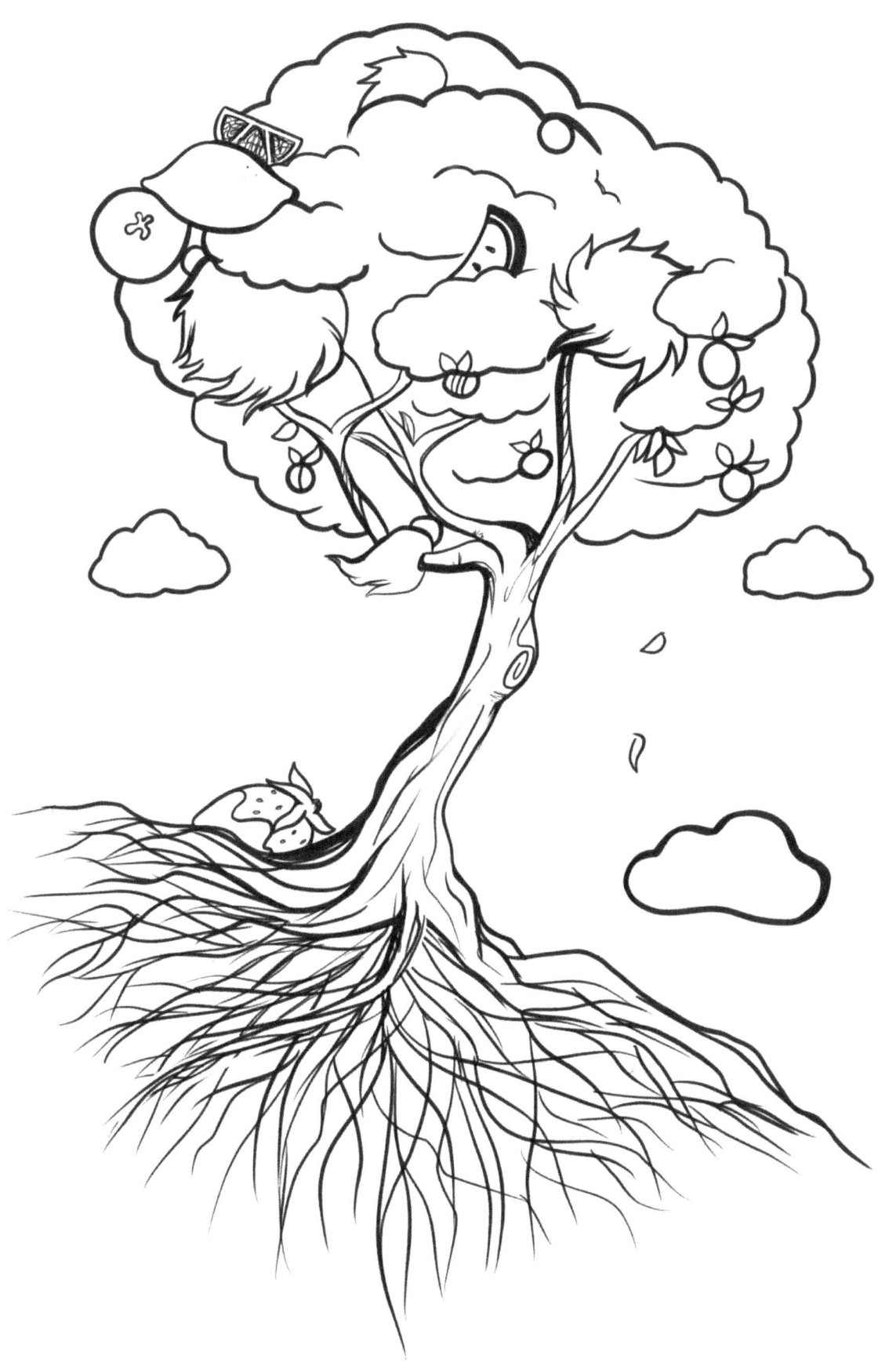

Won Fruit
Two Fruit
Red Fruit
Blue Fruit

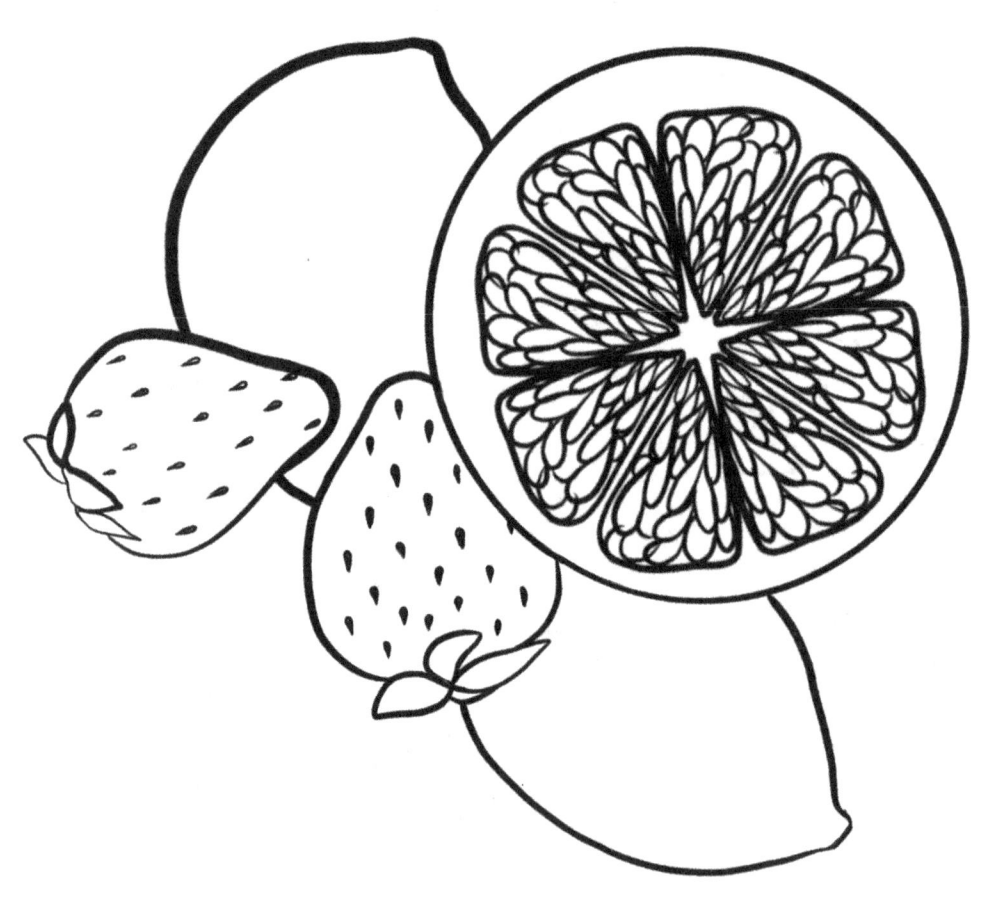

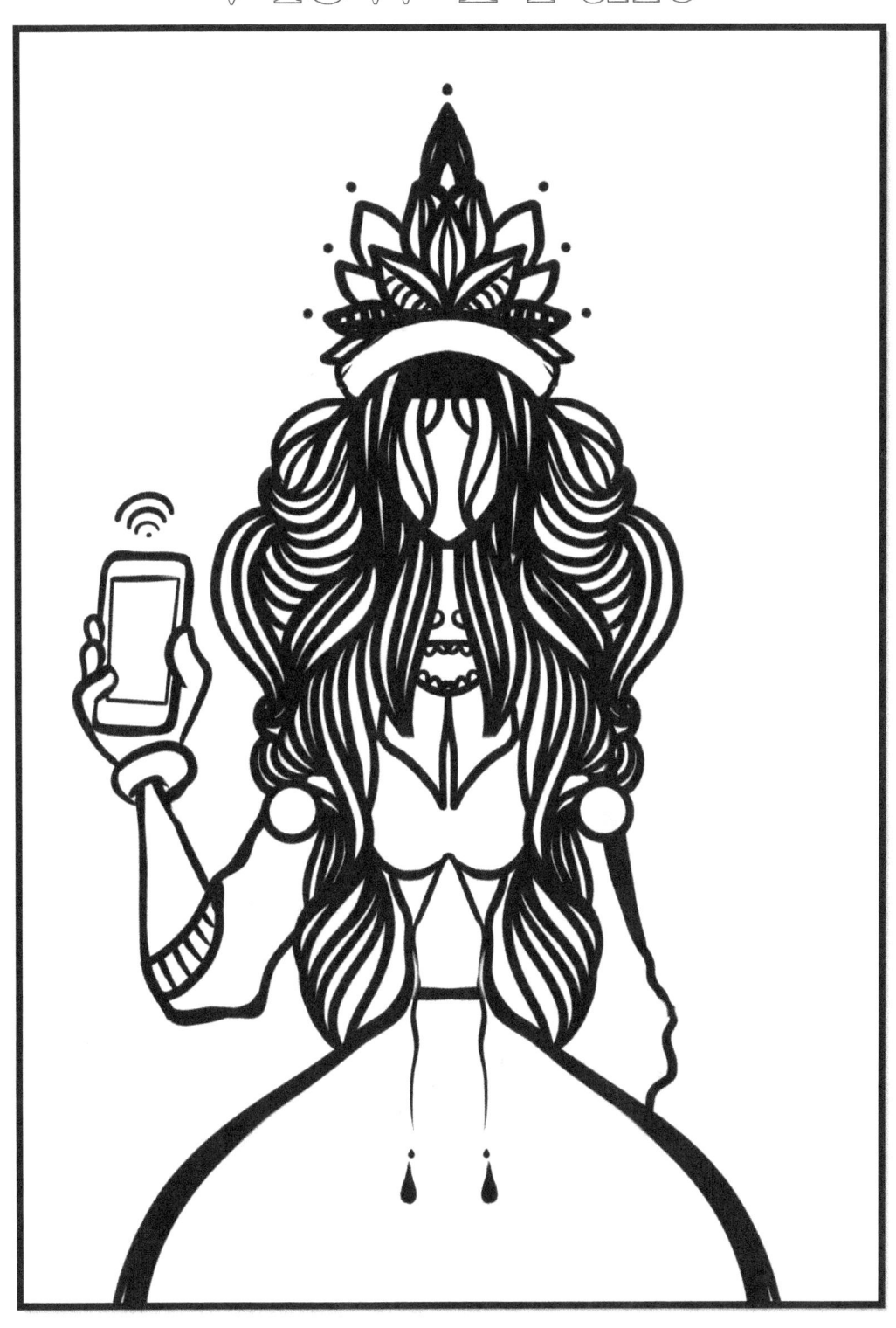

Fresh Fruit
Bad Fruit

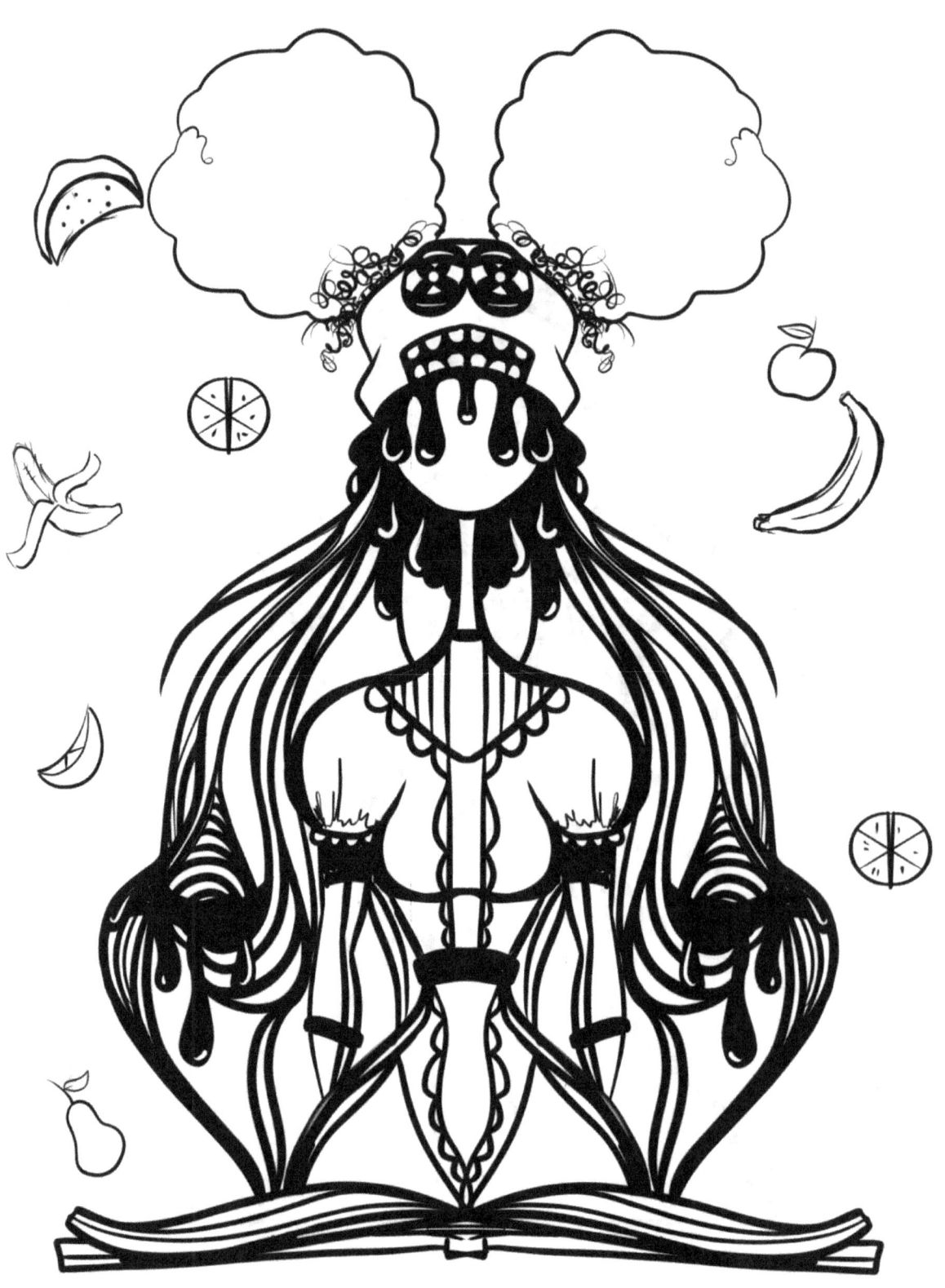

This one is a star.

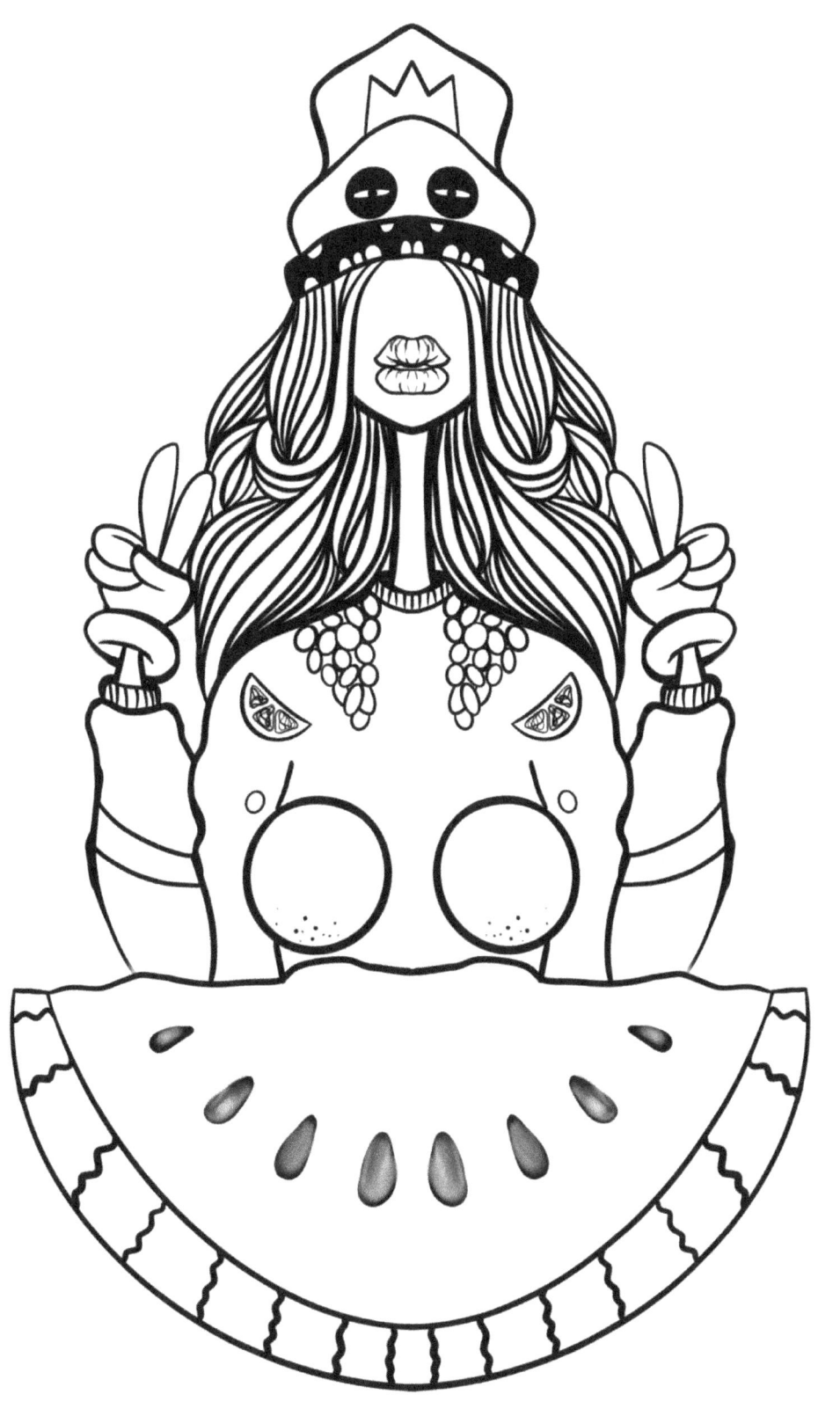

This one has an old school car.

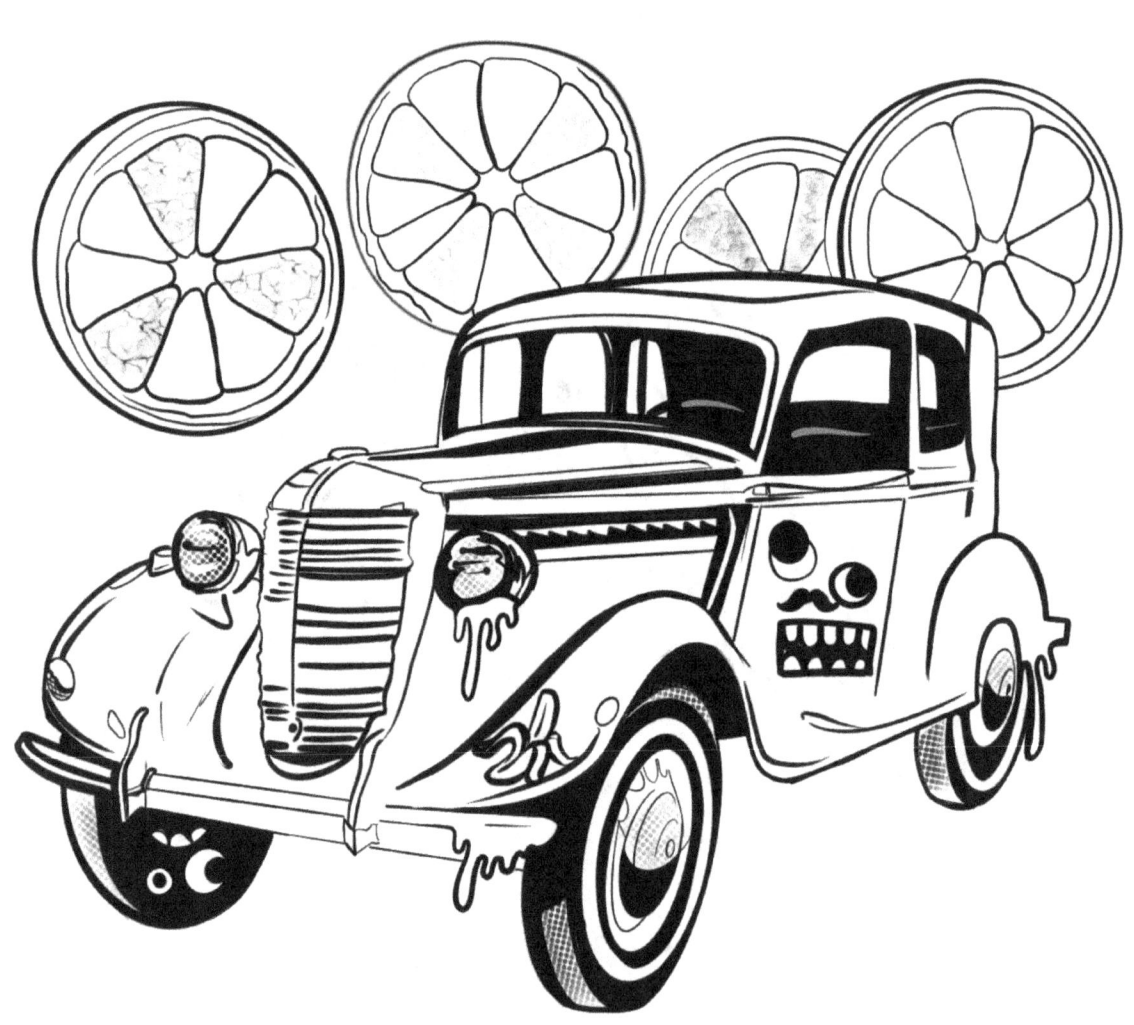

Aye, What a lot of strange fruit there are!

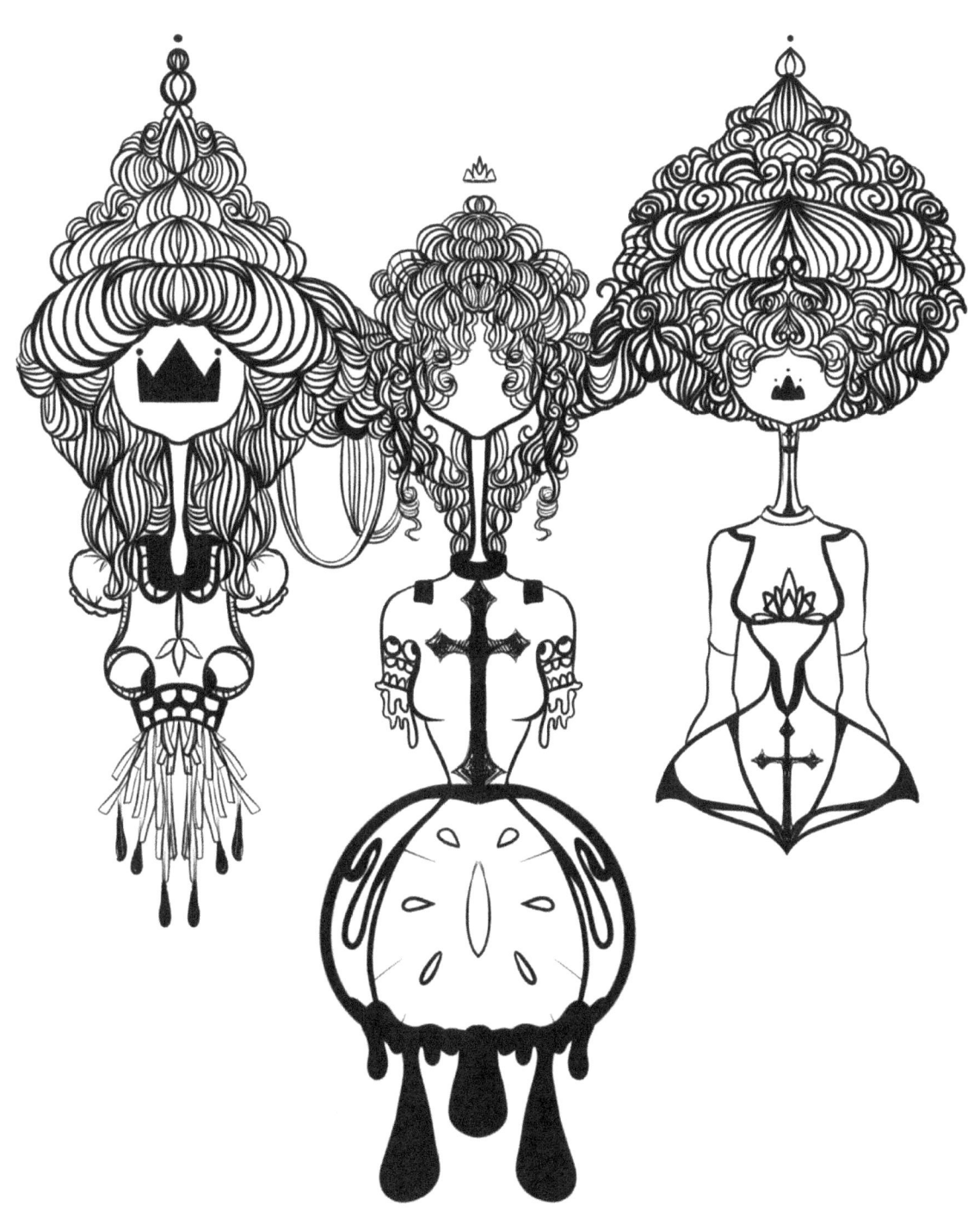

Yes. Some are purple and some are green.

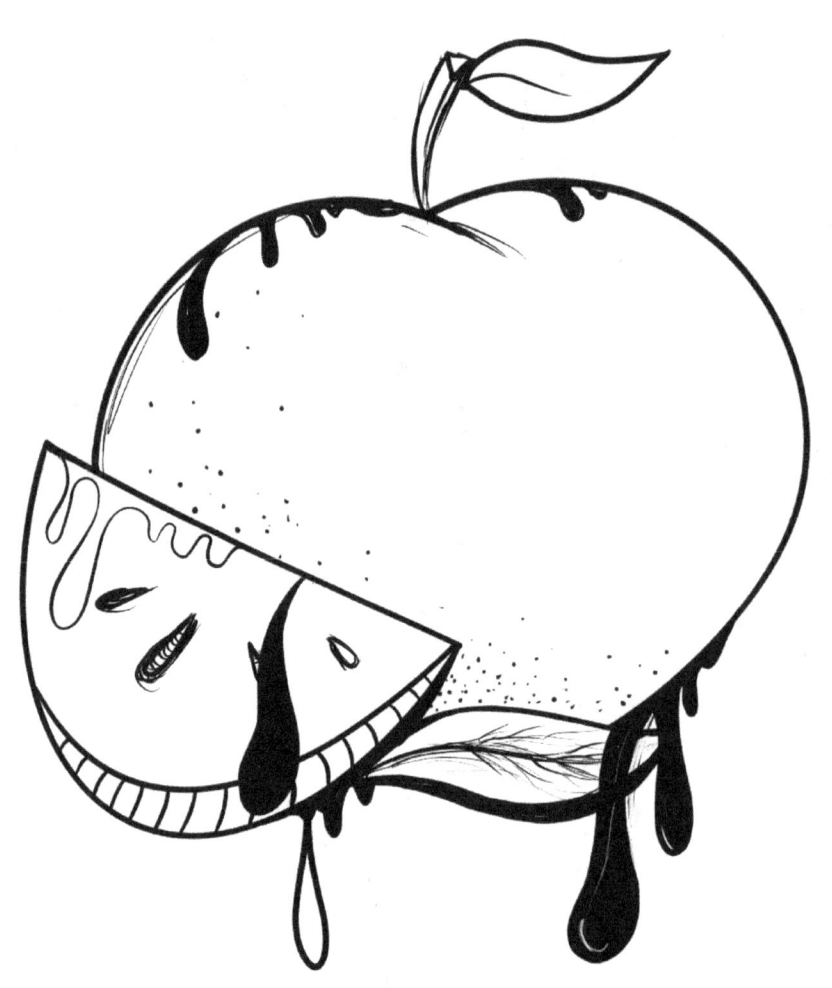

Some are nice and
some are mean.

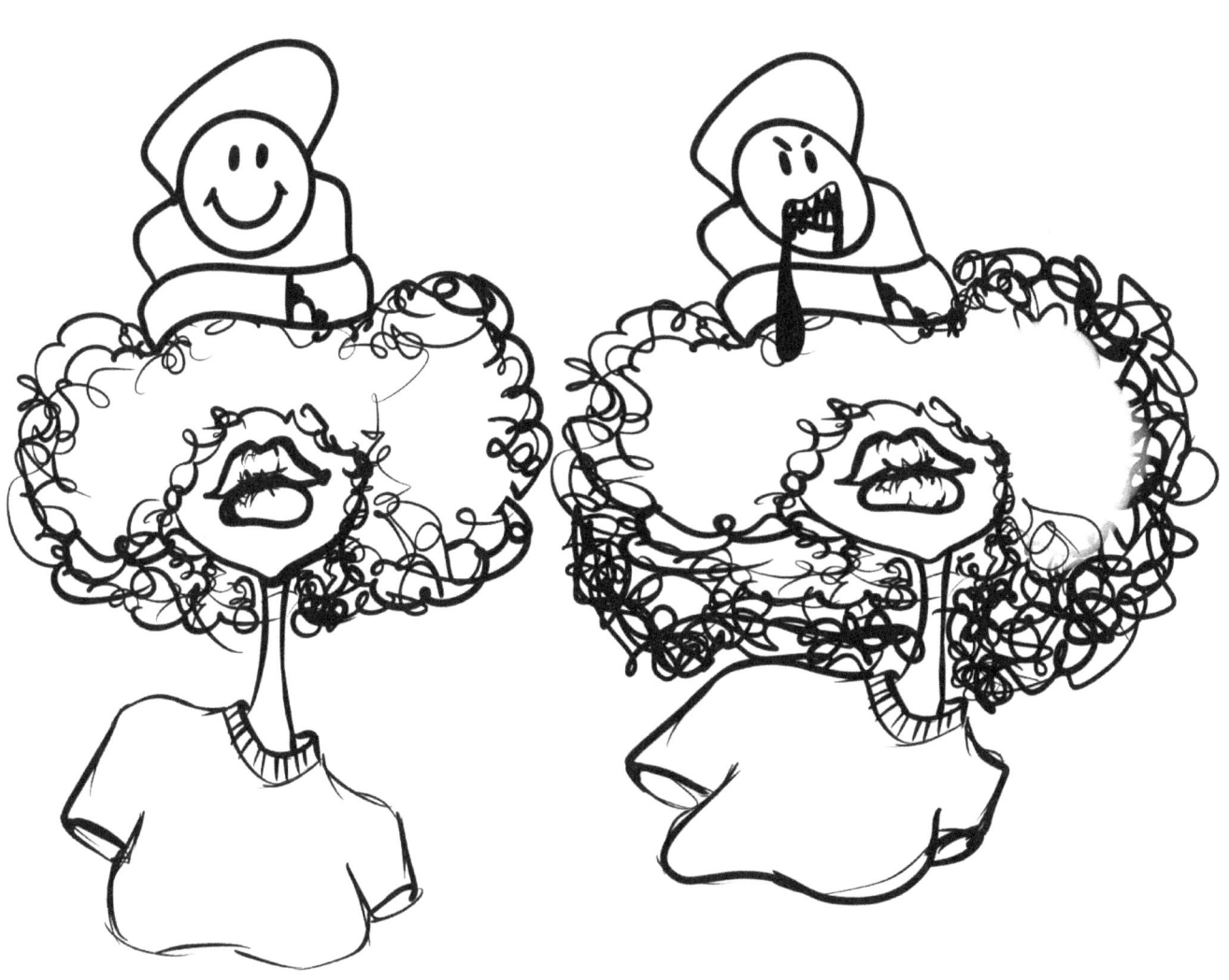

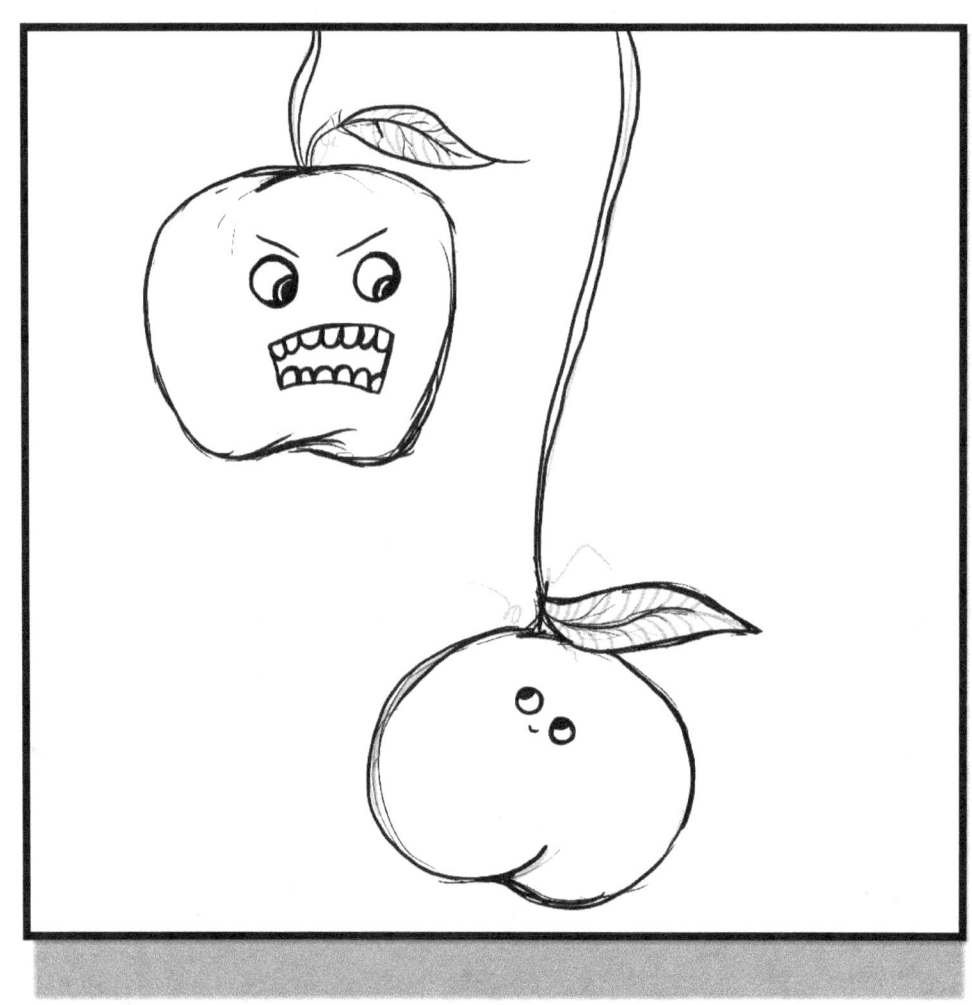

Some are glad,
some sad.
Some are fairly mad.
Why are they sad and
glad and mad?

It is as strange and as simple as a
Lily pad.

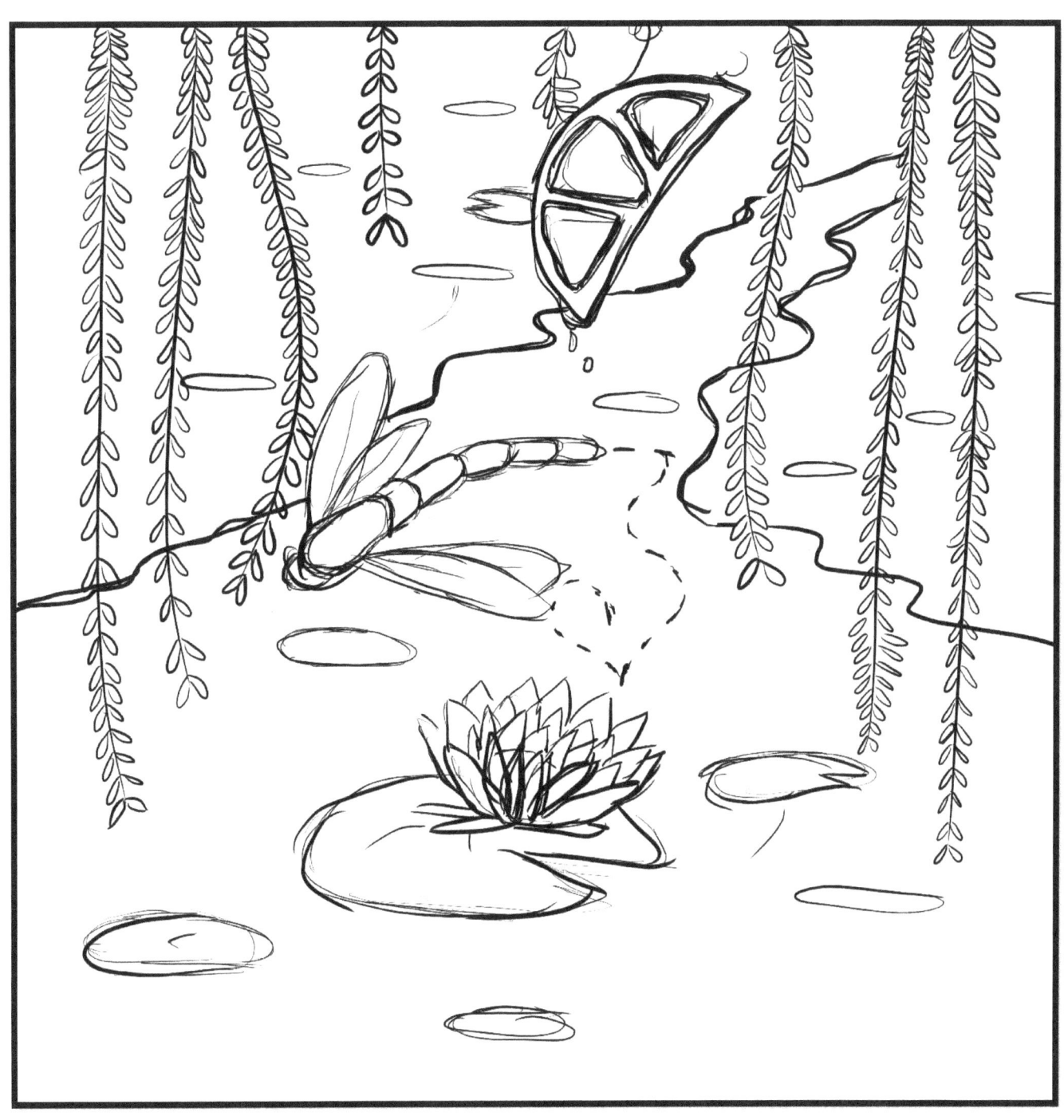

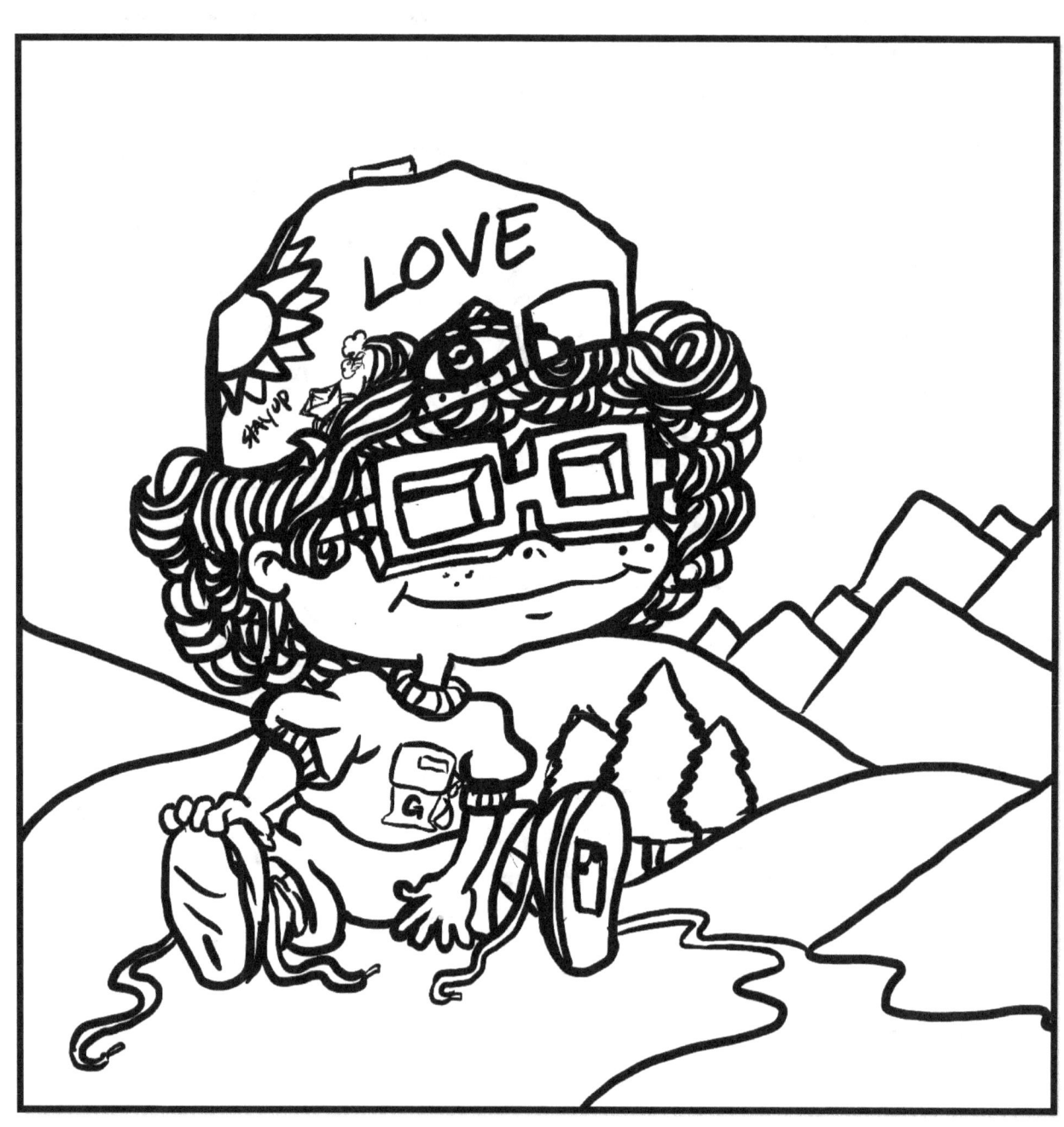

Some are woke.
Some are sleep.

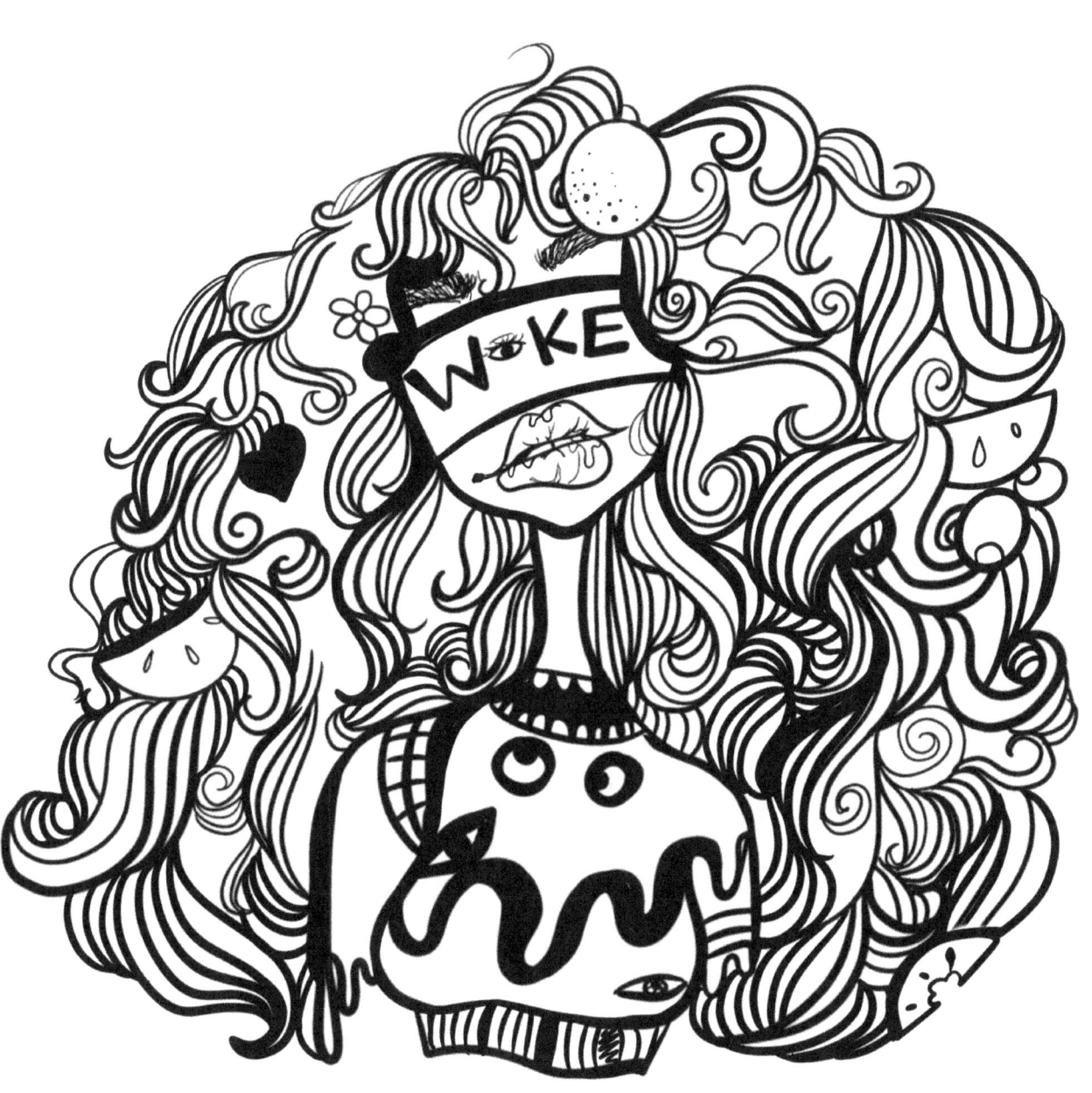

The conscious ones are meek

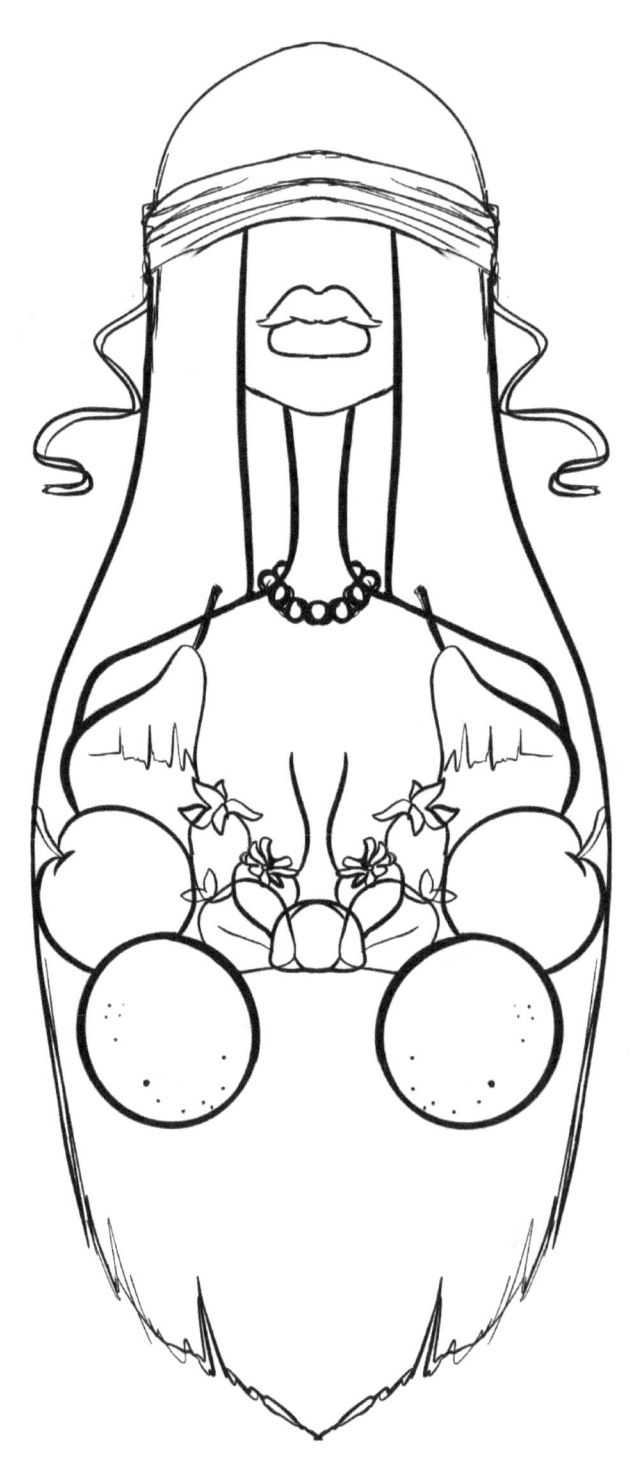

Some are sweet.
Some are bitter.

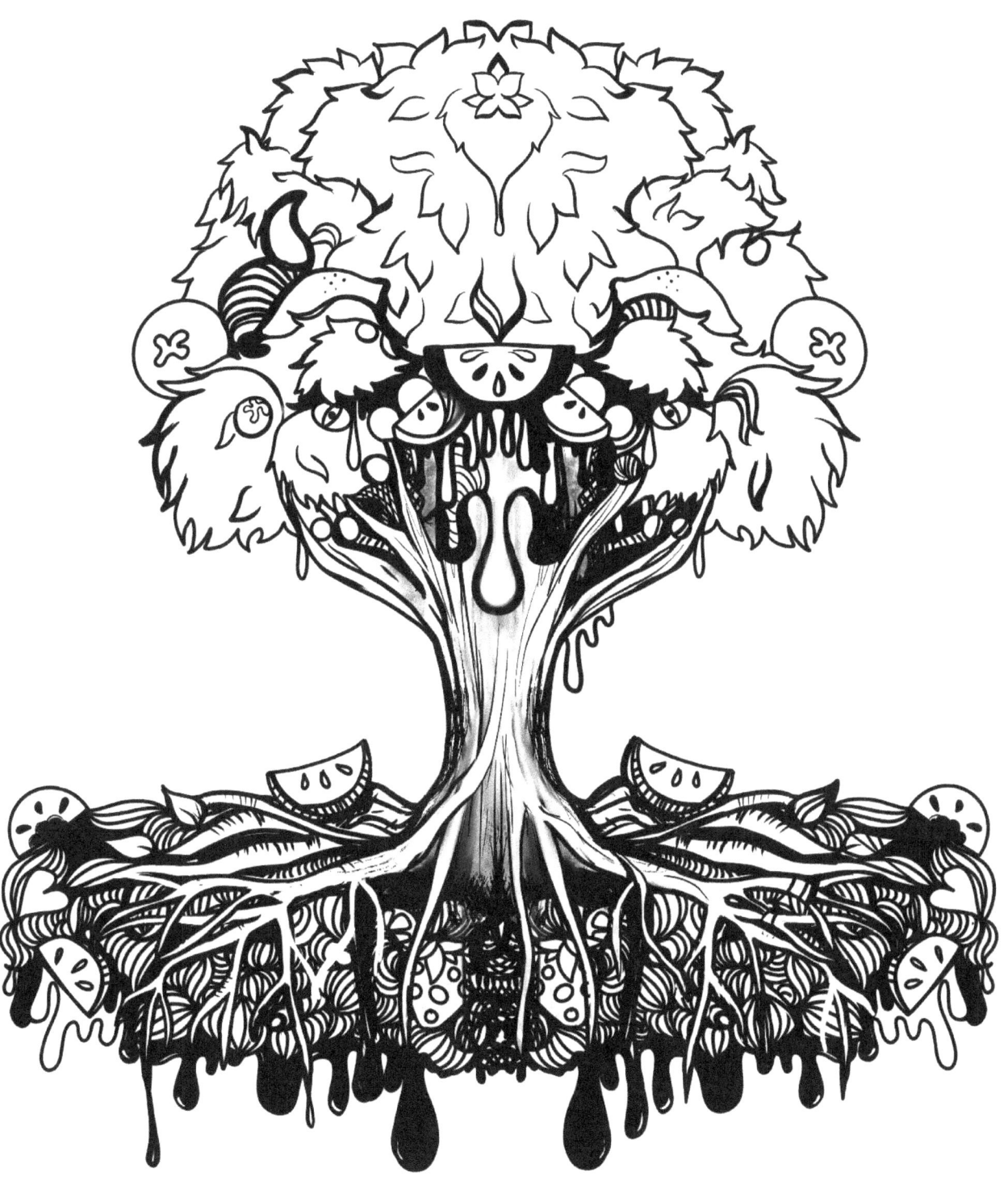

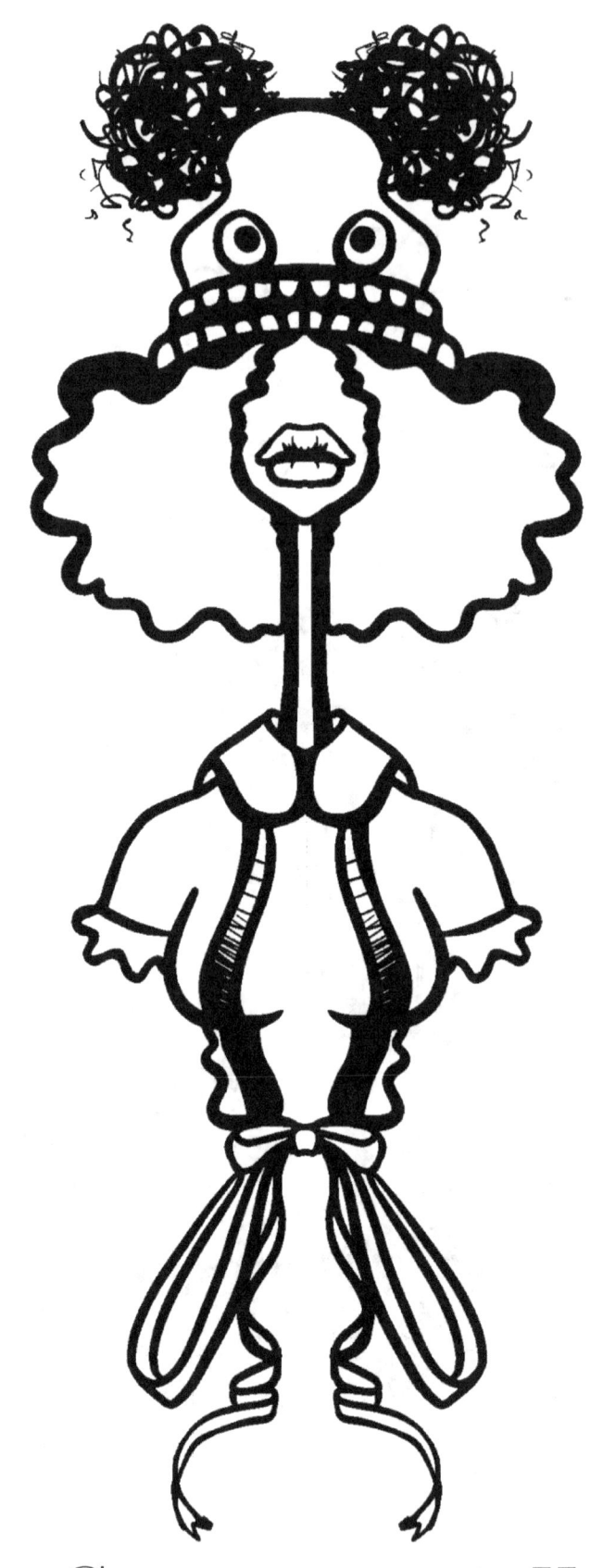

Some may talk
Yet most don't speak

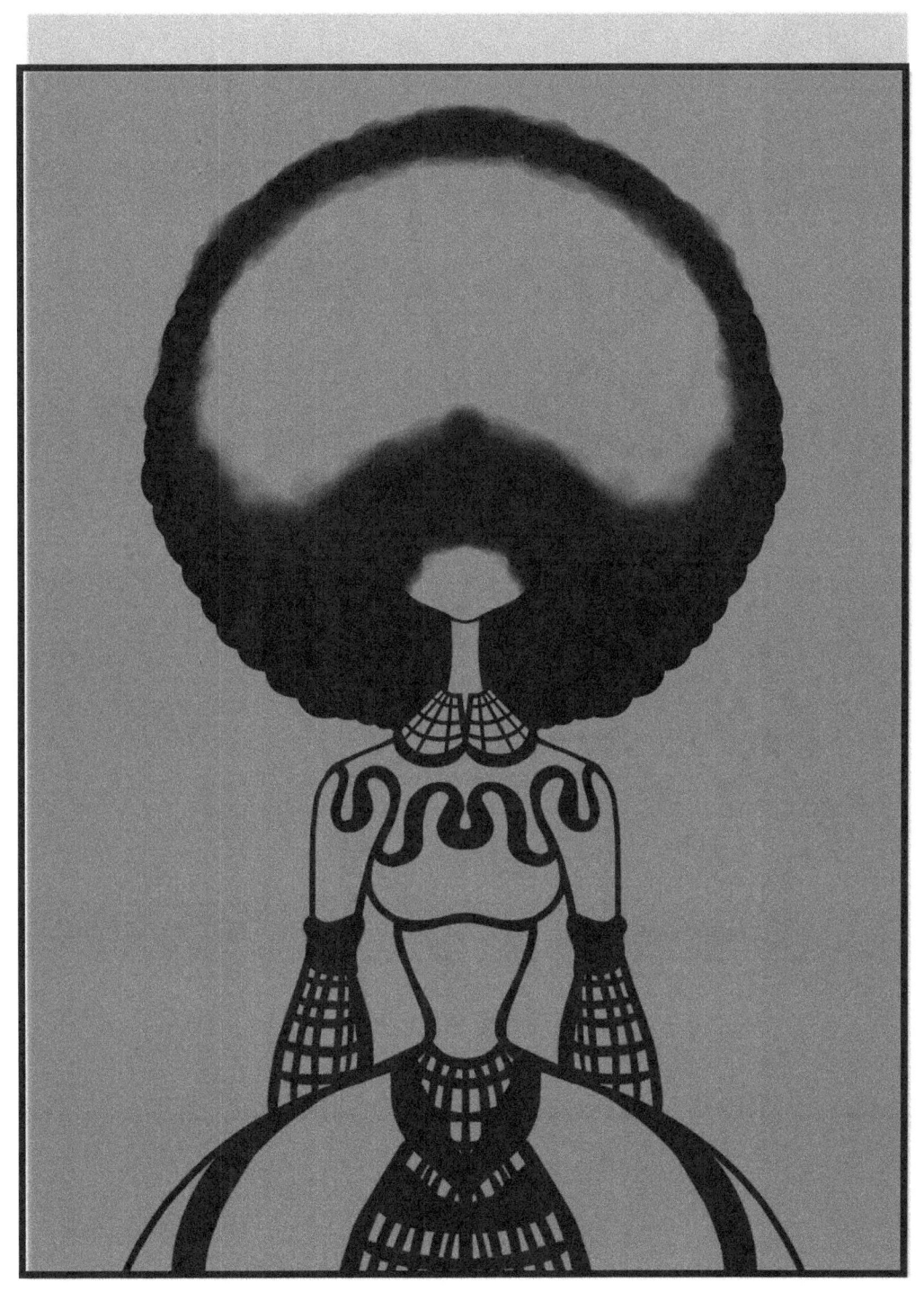

From fear?
Maybe.

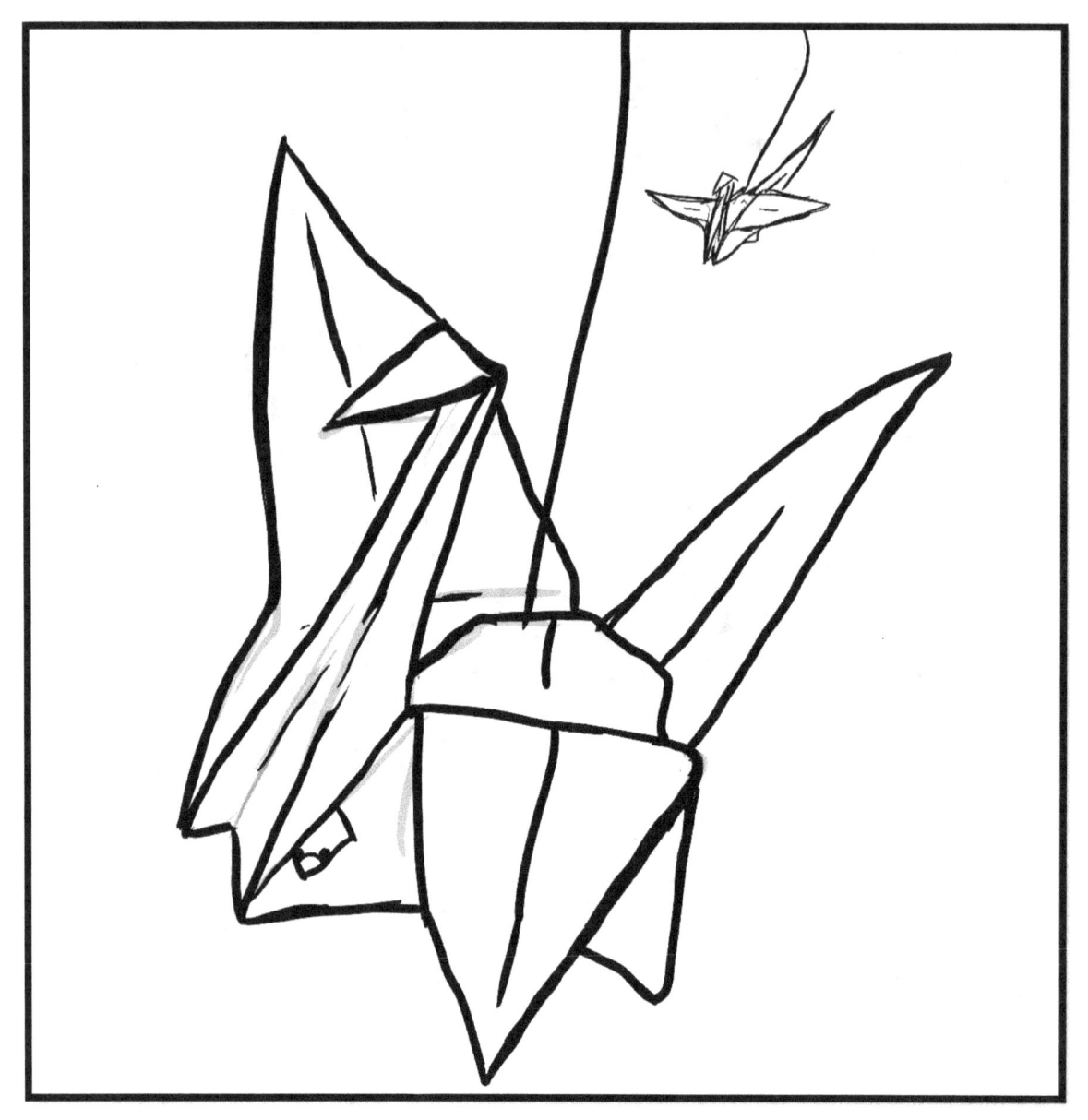

Here are some that like to swing.

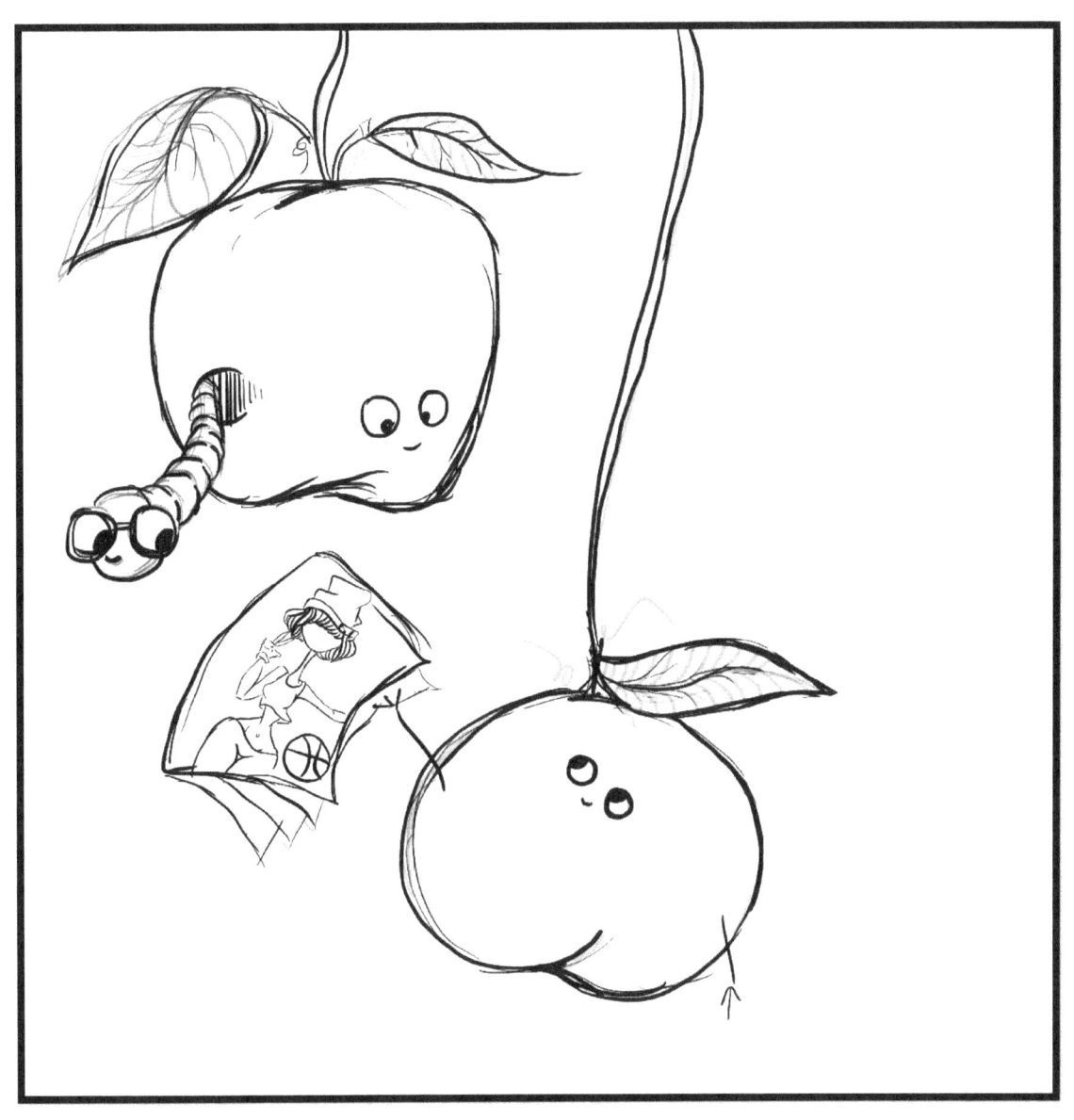

They swing to sing.
Singing and swinging is
a therapeutic thing.

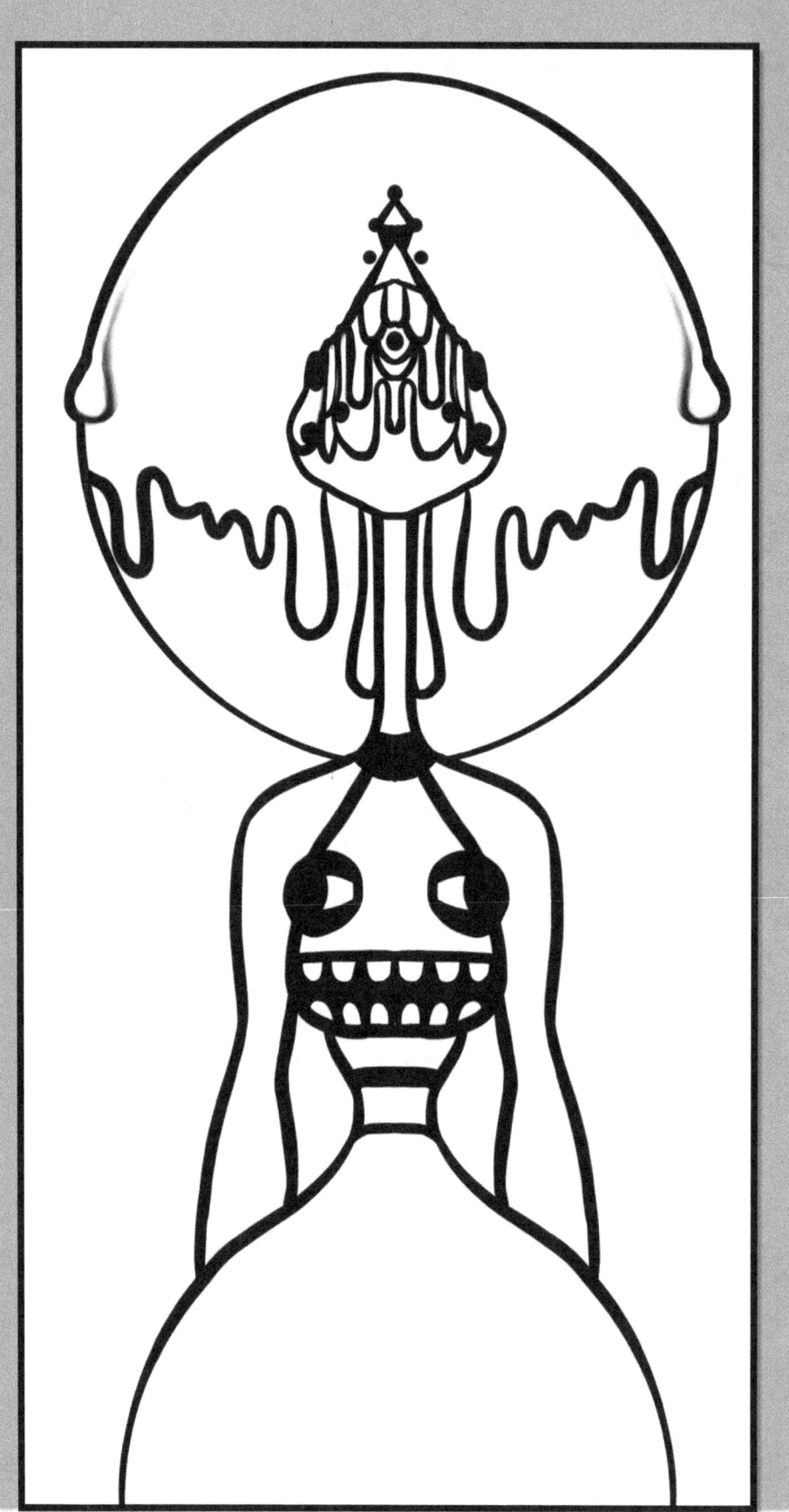

Where do they grow from?
Do we know?

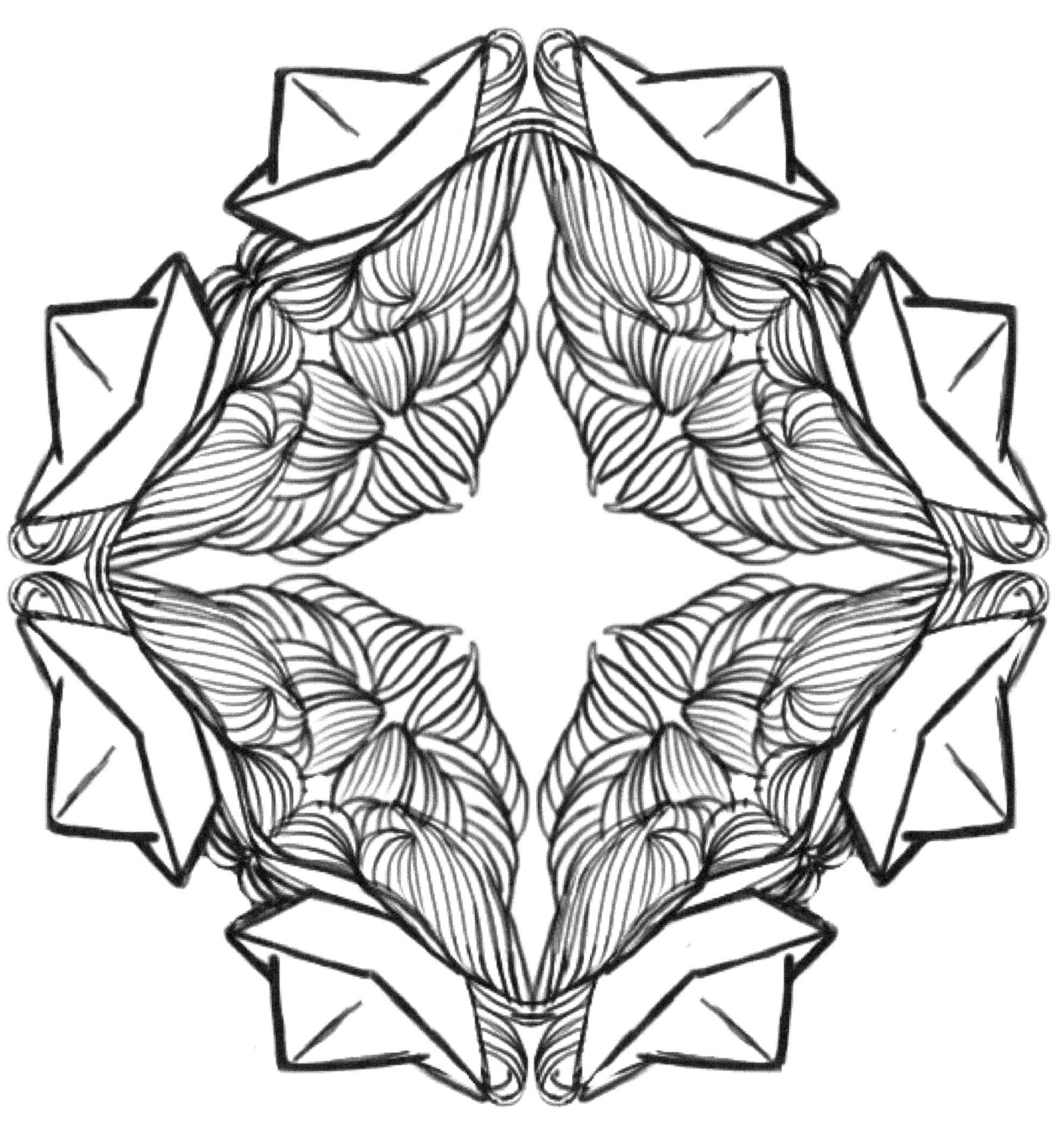

Some have two eyes
And some have more

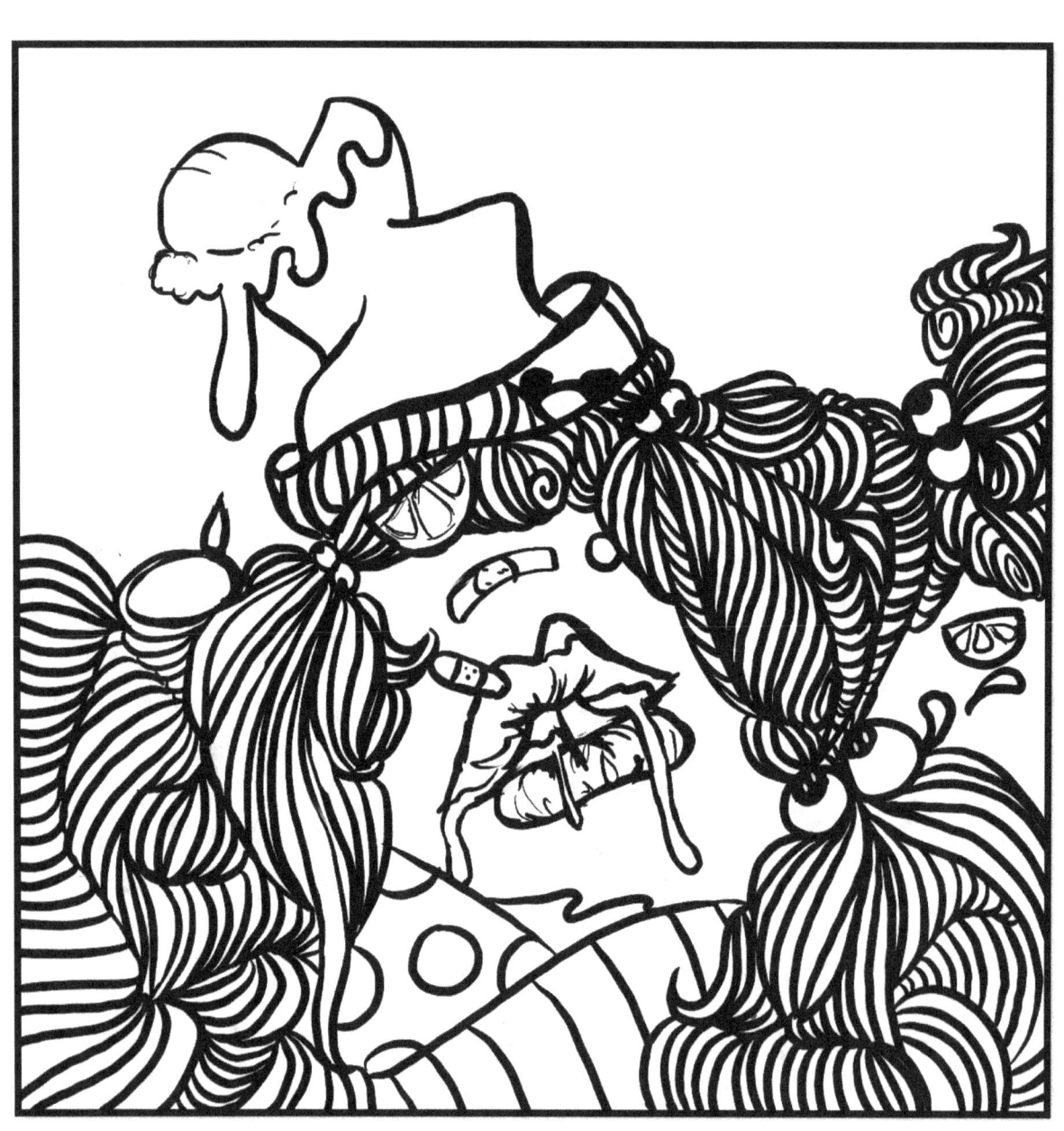

Some have no sight
And remain pour

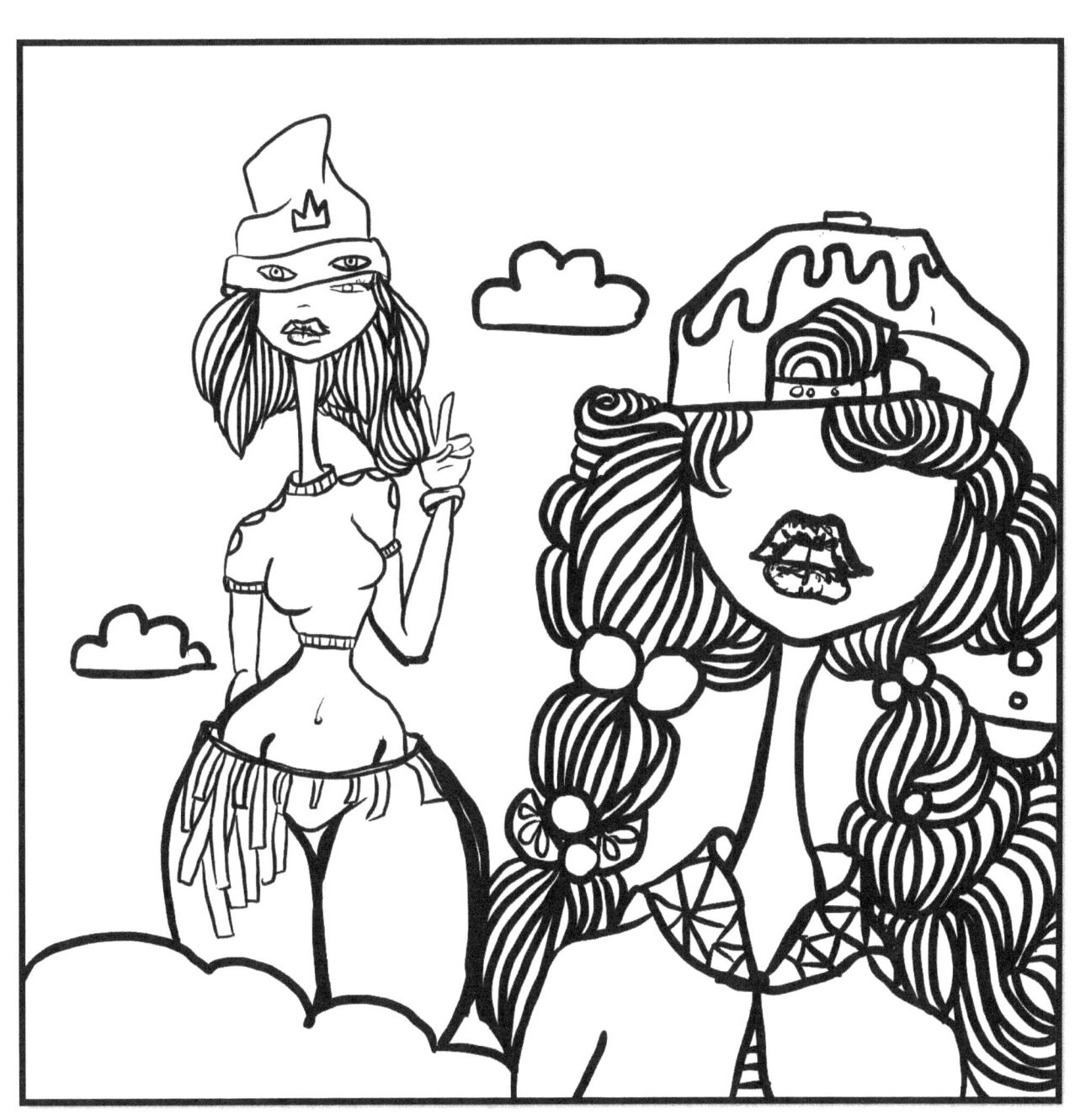

Some are low.

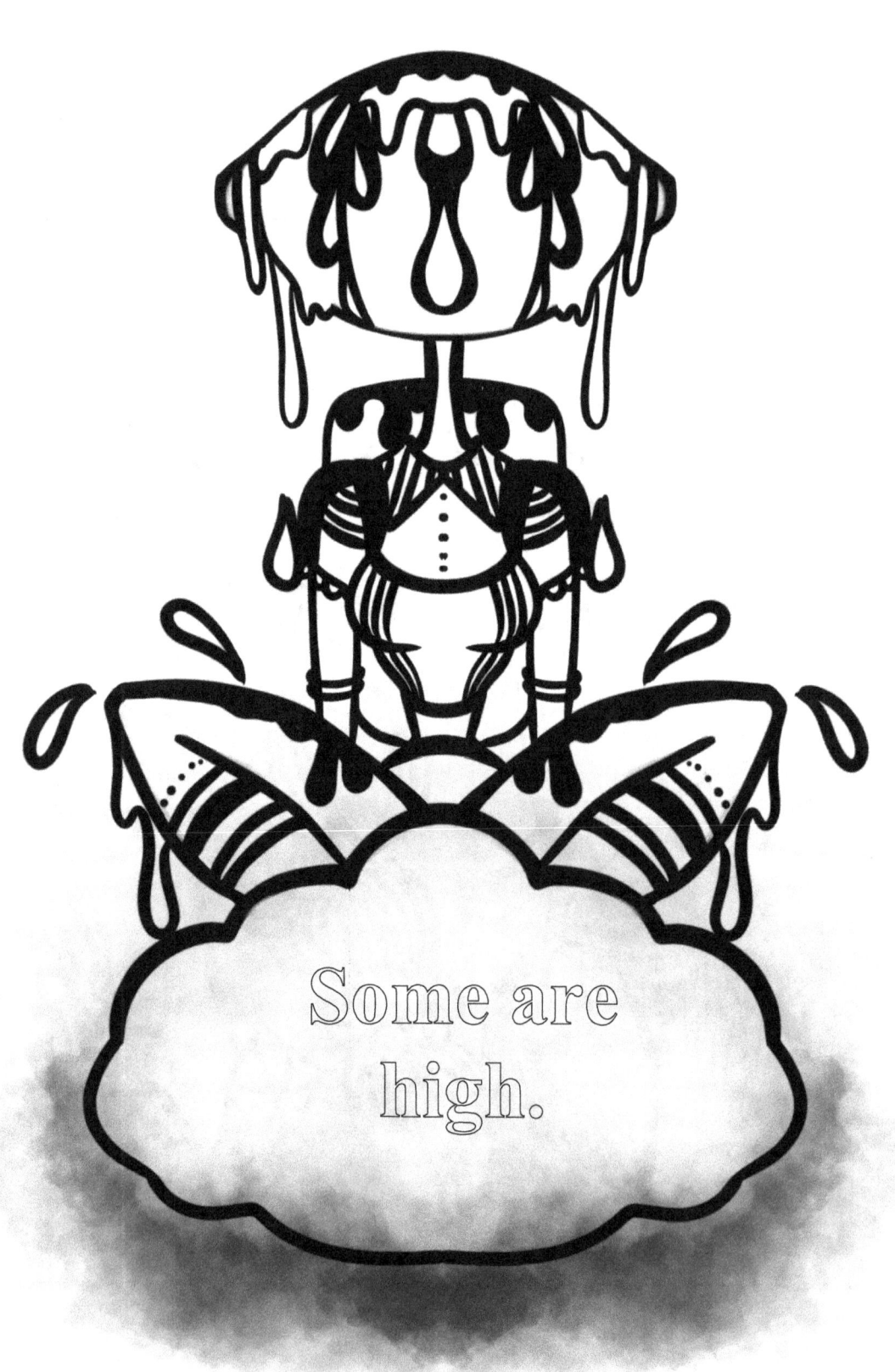

Some are
high.

I assure you strange fruit
grows in strange ways

However, not one of them is
quite the same.

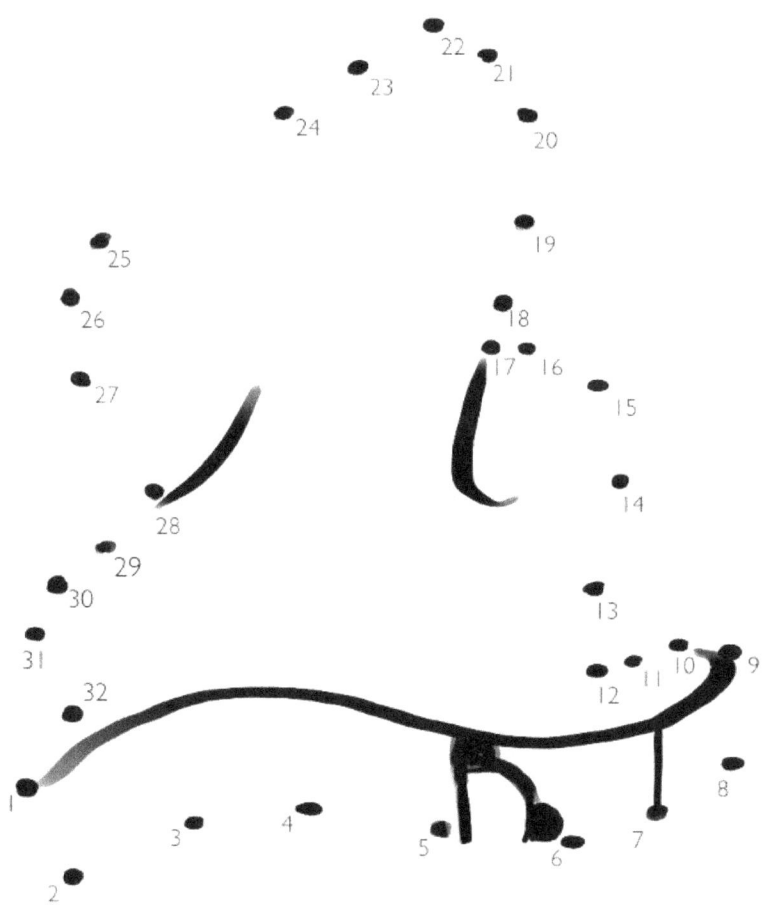

Connect the Dots

Be careful of the Strange crows

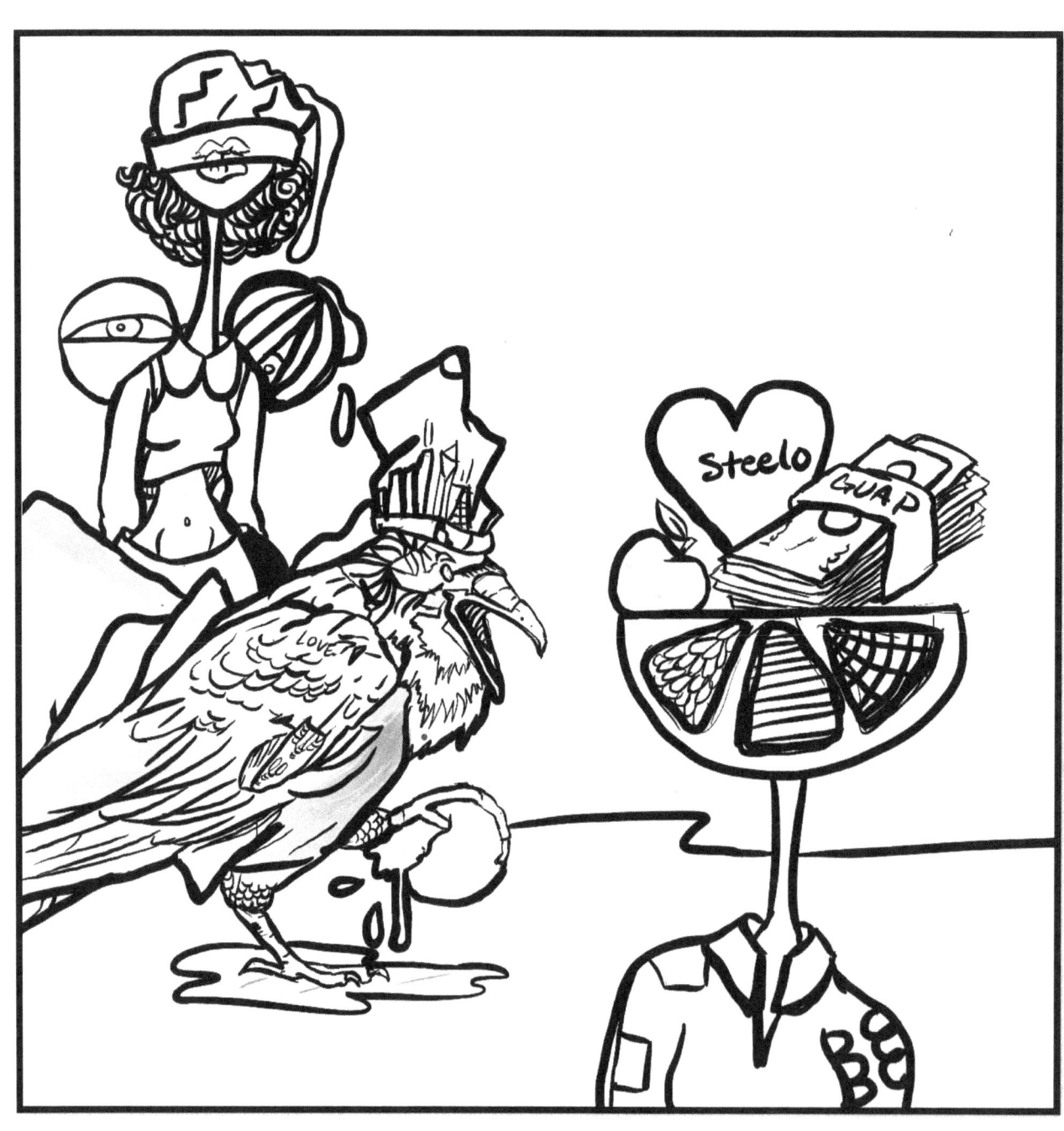

Strange people
gather 'round.

To see the strange fruit
in the summer breeze

Blood Oranges
on the poplar trees.

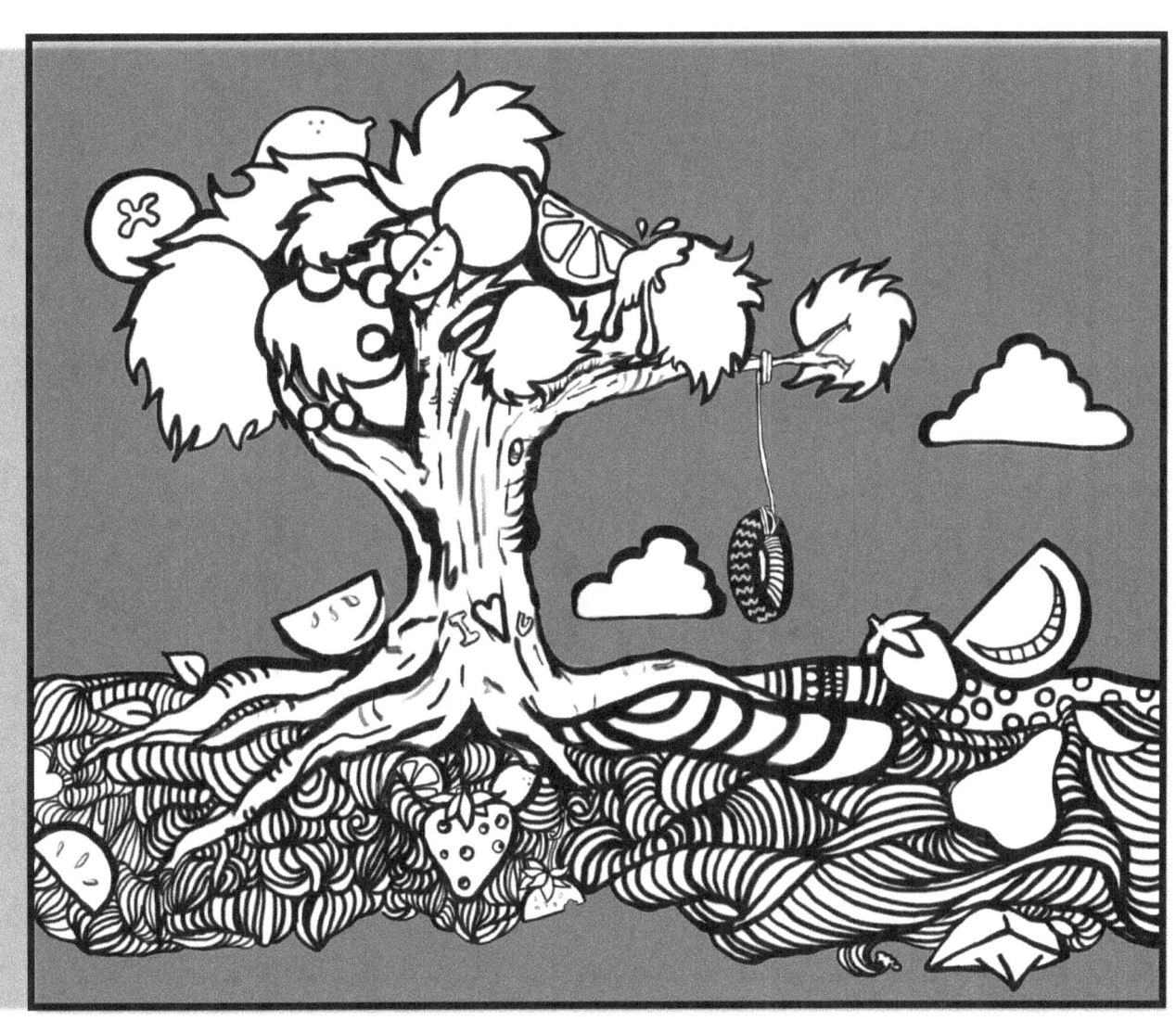

STAY UP

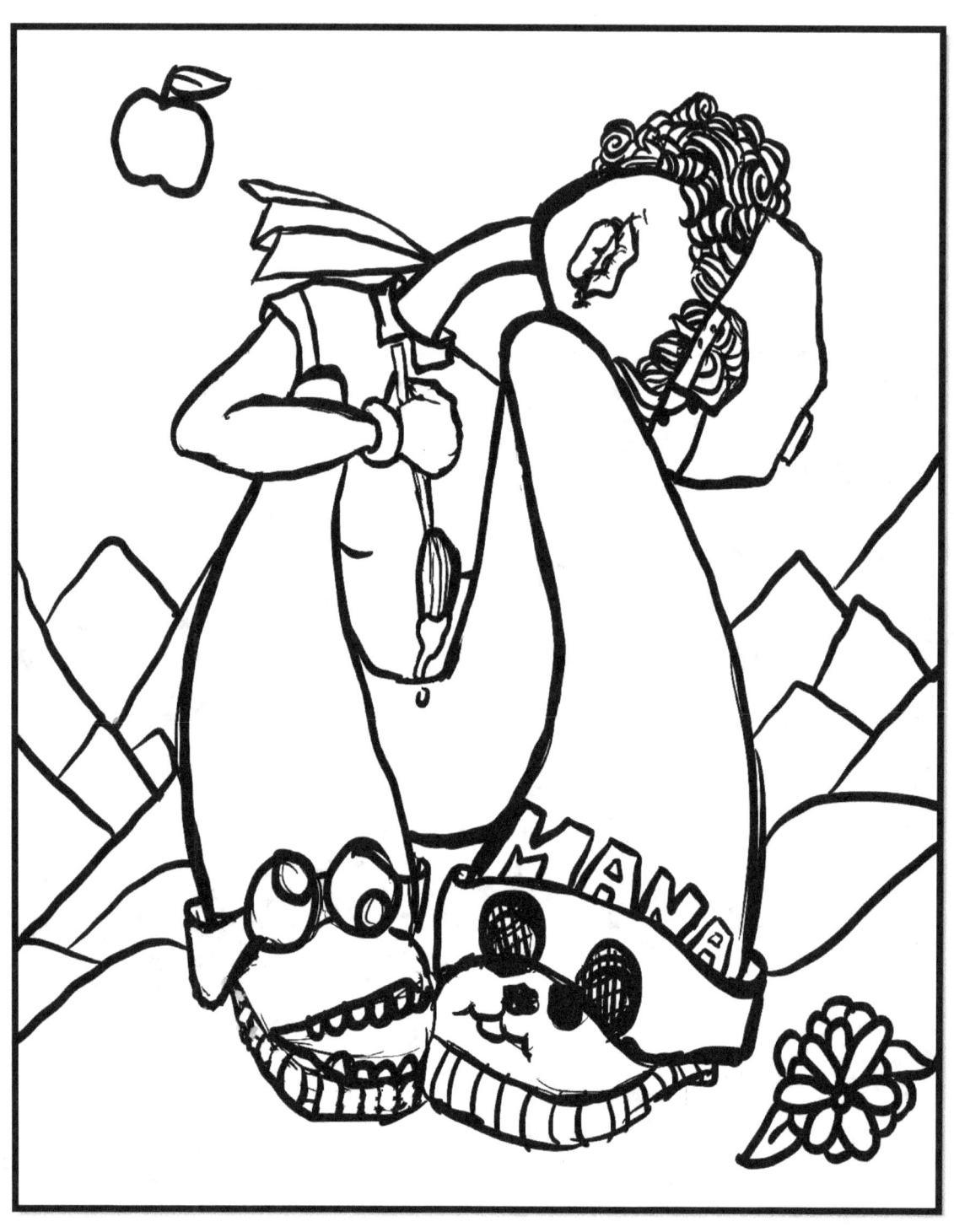